This book is belong to

Color Test

Color Test

Color Test

If you want the best the world has to offer offer the world your best.

In a strong relationship you should love your companion more than you need them.

It's the possibility of having a dream come true that makes life interesting

If my life is going to mean anything, I have to live it myself.

The mind is its own place, and in itself can make a heaven of hell, a hell of heaven.

Happiness is not something ready made. It comes from your own actions

Better to be strong than pretty and useless.

Life is a shipwreck but we must not forget to sing in the lifeboats.

Even if you are on the right track, you'll get run over if you just sit there.

Maybe everyone can live beyond what they're capable of

If you think you are too small to make a difference, try sleeping with a mosquito

Go on with what your heart tells you, or you will lose all

It does not matter how slowly you go as long as you do not stop.

It does not matter how slowly you go as long as you do not stop

Don't think of all the misery but of the beauty that still remains

Keep your face always toward the sunshine and shadows will fall behind you

There is no good and evil, there is only power and those too weak to seek it.

I never want to change so much that people can't recognize me.

Made in the USA
San Bernardino, CA
30 May 2018